Competency Quotient
Leveraging Human Capital
Metrics for Competency Assessment

SUDHIR WARIER

Copyright © 2011 Sudhir Warier

Patent Pending – 3230/MUM/2011

All rights reserved.

ISBN: 1502863456
ISBN-13: 978-1502863454

To all Human Capital Managers ....

CONTENTS

	List of Tables	ii
	List of Figures	iii
	Preface	v
1	**Background**	2
2	**Intangible Assets Management**	6
3	**Competency Quotient**	11
	Key Terms	21
	References	22
	Index	23
	About the Author	25

LIST OF TABLES

Table 1 - Top Ten Human Resource Challenges *7*

Table 2 - CQ – Ranking of Primary Constituents *13*

Table 3 - Academic Value Index - Constituents & Weightage *17*

Table 4 - Employment Value Index *18*

LIST OF FIGURES

Figure 1 – Understanding Competency   3

Figure 2 – Competency vs. Competence   4

Figure 3 – Knowledge Management Framework   8

Figure 4 – Knowledge Management Framework   9

Figure 5 – Competency Quotient – Primary Constituents   12

Figure 6 – Academic Value Index   17

SUDHIR WARIER

PREFACE

The rational approach for business enterprises to survive and gain competitive advantage, in the new world order, is through the continuous development of competencies of their employees. Competitive advantage depends on the ability to effectively activate and use organizational resources. This has led organizations to analyze their internal capabilities with a specific focus on employee's competencies. To effectively harness organizations intangible assets a futuristic, dynamic and proactive approach to competency modelling explicitly aligned with strategic business needs and oriented to its success in the long run, is required. Competency Quotient (CQ) provides a holistic measure of an ascertaining the value of an employee to an organization irrespective of its operational domain. CQ can also be employed to grade fresh graduates being churned out by educational institutions. This is especially of immense value in the Indian subcontinent where there is a tremendous gap between academic curriculum and industry demands.

Sudhir Warier

```
         ┌─────────────────────────┐
         │      Knowledge          │
         │   ╱         ╲           │
         │  Competence             │
         │ Attitude    Skills      │
         └─────────────────────────┘
```

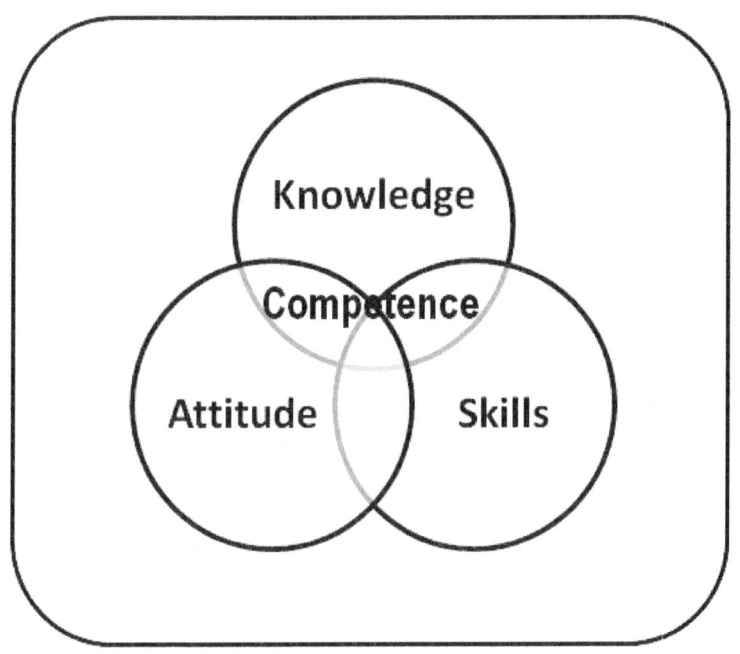

"The only true wisdom is in knowing you know nothing."
Socrates

1 BACKGROUND

In the current highly competitive knowledge based economies, optimal harnessing of its intellectual resources has become a key factor that differentiates successful organizations from the others. The highly challenging, competitive and dynamic business landscape necessitates the use of talent management strategies and is becoming a critical business goal that can help organizations retain their competitive edge and sustain their leadership positions. Talent Management refers to the entire gamut of activities including attracting, nurturing, developing, rewarding and retaining the corporate workforce. Talent Management encompasses the recruiting and staffing, learning & development, performance management, compensation management and career/succession planning functions and has to be supported by organizational competency management and assessment initiatives.

In response to the changes in the business landscape, organizations have become flexible, receptive to the ever changing needs of the customer, cost conscious, environment friendly while adopting a flatter and leaner management structures. However business enterprises soon realized that in continuously volatile economic & technology environment the only way to survive and gain competitive advantage is through the continuous development of competencies of their employees. Competitive advantage depends on the ability to effectively activate and use organizational resources. This has led organizations to analyze their internal capabilities with a specific focus on employee's competencies. To effectively harness organizations intangible assets a futuristic, dynamic and proactive approach to competency modelling explicitly aligned with strategic business needs and oriented to its success in the long run, is required.

What is Competency or What are Competencies?

Competencies can be defined as the cognitive, affective, behavioural and motivational personality or dispositions of an individual enabling him/her to perform well in specific situations. Thus competency can be defined as "The knowledge, skills and attributes (KSA) that differentiates superior performers from others in every sphere of life. The development of accurate and appropriate competencies results in enhanced organizational learning, performance management while maximizing the usage of the organizational intangible assets. The concept is summarized in figure 1.

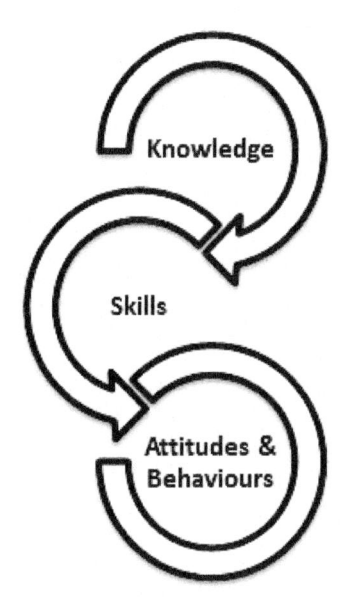

Figure 1 – Understanding Competency

Competence versus Competency – The Differentiators

It may be noted that the dictionary meaning of the terms 'Competence' and 'Competency' are identical. However the context of application is entirely different and hence the terms have different meaning in their respective domains. The term 'Competency' is used in the context of an 'individual' while 'Competence' is used from an organizational perspective. This implies that the terms 'Competency Management' and 'Competence Management' are distinct and involve different set of entities – An Individual, Organization. The primary differences between the terms is summarized and graphically presented in figure 2.

COMPETENCY

Core Behaviours
- Intrinsic
- Generic
- Individual Excellence
- KSAB of Top Performers

Add-on/Acquired Characteristics
- Extrinsic
- Job Specific
- Organizational Excellence
- Deliver consistenent & Optimal Performance

COMPETENCE

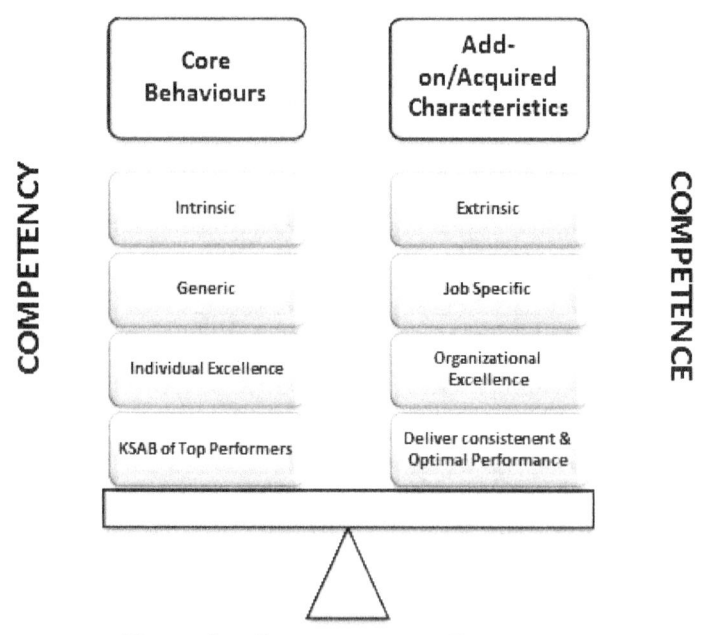

Figure 2 – Competency vs. Competence

Competency refers to the intrinsic knowledge, skills, attitudes and behaviours (KSAB) of top performers irrespective of the domain, discipline, industry or institution. Thus competencies are defined from an individual perspective and refer to their inborn traits and behaviours. Competencies can be polished, sharpened or honed through suitable learning interventions. Competency

COMPETENCY QUOTIENT

Management involves identification, extraction of KSAB of top performers (typically top 5% of a group) and replicating them in others through suitable Learning & Development (most popular) interventions. *Competencies can be defined as knowledge, skills, mind-sets and, thought patterns resulting in successful performance* (Dubois, 1998).

The term Competence is used in the context of enhancing organizational performance. *Competence refers to the critical skills, knowledge and, associated best practices specific to definite tasks leading to optimal accomplishment of organizational goals or enhanced organizational performance* (Gilbert, 1996). Competence can be enhanced or acquired through suitable interventions including on-the-job training (OTJ), Learning & Development (L&D) activities and are job specific and focussed on enhancing organizational excellence.

A modern day simplified definition of Competence would be "The knowledge, skills and contextual background required by an individual to meet and exceed his/her organizational Key Result Areas (KRA's). Competence Management encompasses all tools, techniques, methods and procedures employed by organizations to assess the available skill sets of its workforce and mapping it in accordance to its current and future requirements. Competence Management involves an organizational need and benefits analysis, competency definition, competency assessment, model building, evaluation and deployment with the sole objective of leveraging the Intellectual Capital (IC) to bring about a sustainable competitive advantage and tangible benefits to the organization.

Human capital (HC) is the collection of intangible resources that are embedded in the members of the organization. These resources can be of three main types:
1. *Competencies and Competence* (including skills and know-how)
2. *Attitude* (motivation, leadership qualities of the top management)
3. *Intellectual Agility* (the ability of members to adapt to changing organizational landscape)

2 INTANGIBLE ASSETS MANAGEMENT

Competency Management (CM) activities are complex to understand as well as implement primarily due to the fact that competencies are confusing and needs to be viewed from the people/employee perspective. Organizations needs to understand their core competency requirements on the technical as well as the personal (behavioural) front, identify the behaviours of their best performers and finally duplicate them to drive higher productivity at all levels of the organization.

Another important aspect is that competency descriptions are not uniformly specified nor defined across at the national/international, sectoral or organizational levels. This leads to an opaque competency description market with a multitude of competency frameworks and competency benchmarks. Thus there would not be any uniformity in competency definitions among peer organizations of the member countries within the European Union (EU) or the United States of America (USA). This also implies that there are no standardized ontologies for CM. As a result automated reasoning engines, which utilizes the interrelations between entities to make "intelligent" choices in different situations within the domain, cannot be designed and deployed. This also implies that automated tools such as skill gap analysis, training need analysis (TNA), job search and recruitment based on individual semantically

specified competency descriptions cannot be developed. The major problem with defining a common ontology for competencies is that there are so many viewpoints of competencies and competency frameworks. A comprehensive research undertaken by Bersin & Associates covering over 700 global corporations have identified the following eight challenges in organizational talent management. They are as listed below:
1. Workforce planning
2. Performance management
3. Competency management
4. Leadership development
5. Succession planning
6. Learning and development
7. Compensation
8. Talent Management Software Systems

Further, another survey of over 200 senior Human Resource (HR) professionals from private and public enterprises representing 5% of the total workforce in the United Kingdom (UK) have come out with the top ten challenges facing HR professionals. These results validate the findings of the Bersin & Associates research. They key findings are summarized in the table 1 below:

Table 1 – Top Ten Human Resource Challenges

S.N.	PARAMETER	RESPONDENTS (%)
1	Developing high-performing teams	66
2	Succession planning	55
3	Managing talent through change	54
4	Finding/sourcing talent externally	51
5	Developing high potential	48
6	Managing performance	46
7	Engaging people	44
8	Assessing best talent to join organization	43
9	Identifying high potential	43
10	Selecting best for internal moves	42

The figure 3 below depicts the organizational management framework, the key components and their inter-linkages (Warier Sudhir, 2003).

```
                          ┌─────────────────────┐
                          │   Human Capital     │
                          │   Management        │
                          └─────────────────────┘
                                    │
              ┌──────────────┐      │     ┌─────────────────────────┐
              │  Competency  │──────┼─────│  Organizational         │
              │  Management  │            │  Competence/Individual  │
              └──────────────┘            │  Competency             │
                    │                     └─────────────────────────┘
┌──────────────┐    │    ┌──────────────────┐    ┌──────────────┐
│  Knowledge   │────┼────│ Agility (Innovation & │────│ Performance  │
│  Management  │         │    Creativity)   │    │  Management  │
└──────────────┘         └──────────────────┘    └──────────────┘
                                 │
                         ┌──────────────────┐
                         │   Learning &     │
                         │   Development    │
                         └──────────────────┘
```

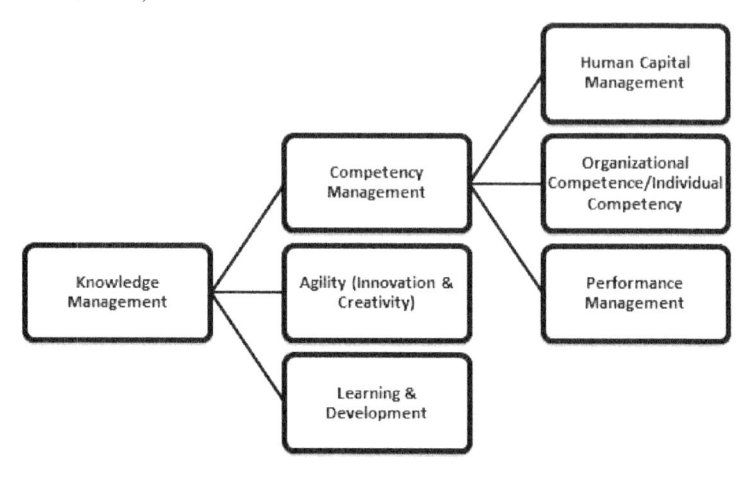

Figure 3 – Knowledge Management Framework

A key measure of organizational intangible assets is its Intellectual Capital (IC) or Knowledge Capital. IC includes all organizational intangible resources as well as their interconnections and refers to the collection of intangible resources and their flows. Intangible assets can be defined as all directly controlled resources that contribute to its value generation. This makes it evident that a concise definition of IC cannot be arrived at since IC is specific to each and every organization. The variables that an organization can and cannot influence depend on many factors. Thus the IC for one organization considers may not be of any use to another organization or is context specific. The overall value of an organization represents its physical and monetary assets (financial capital) as well as its unique collection of intangible resources. The figure 4 illustrates the organizational value chain:

```
                    Organizational Value
                    /              \
            Financial          Intellectual
            Capital            Capital
                               /         \
                        Human           Structural
                        Capital         Capital
                        |               |
                        Competence  —  Relationship
                        |               |
                        Attitude    —  Organization
                        |               |
                        Intellectual —  Renewal &
                        Agility         Development
```

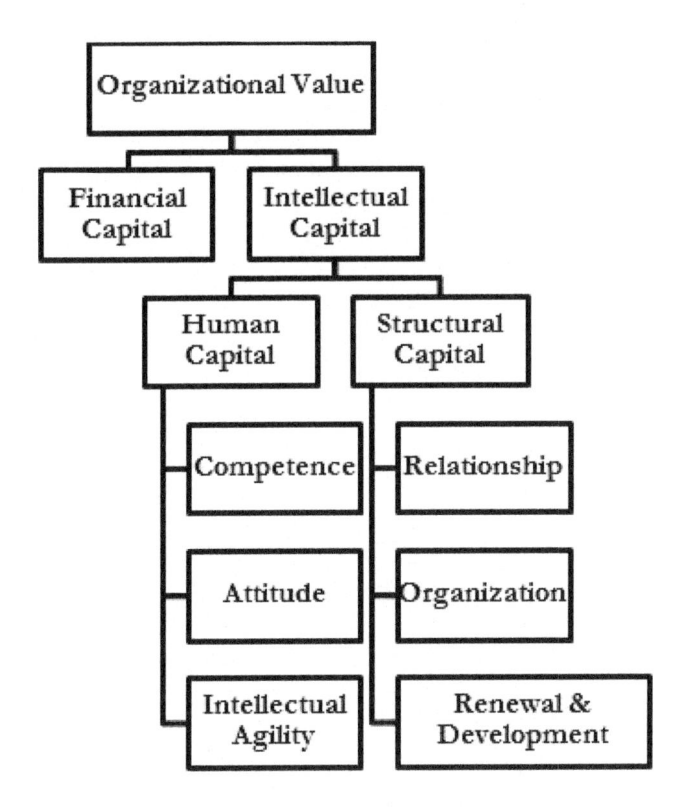

Figure 4 – Knowledge Management Framework

Human capital is the collection of intangible resources that are embedded in the members of the organization. These resources can be of three main types:
    a. Competencies (including skills and know-how)
    b. Attitude (motivation, leadership qualities of the top management)
    c. Intellectual agility (the ability of members to adapt to changing organizational landscape)

The essence of structural capital is the knowledge embedded within the routines of an organization. It comprises all the intangible resources which are the property of the company. This implies that there exists a market for trading in intangible resources in a manner similar to the equity, debt or commodity markets. However such a market would be governed by an entirely different set of characteristics. Identifying the different types of IC can be likened to the identification of stocks of intangible resources. It becomes imperative for an organization to measure and thus manage the flows of IC. The choice of IC indicators should be guided by the long-term strategy of the organization, its vision or mission. Once an organization has clear ideas on its identity and its long-term goal, it should use these goals to identify two sets of variables: one is the "value creating path" - the IC categories or focus areas that really drive value creation and the set of key success factors (KSF) and indicators that are appropriate as performance measurements.

3 COMPETENCY QUOTIENT

Introduction

Typically individual screening within an organization happens prior to recruitment. There is no subsequent evaluation of an individual, in most organizations, during their tenure. This implies that organizations have no record of the progress of an individual during their term, no means of measuring the skills and competencies developed and lost during their tenure, no means of identifying suitable interventions for competency development as well as estimating the return-on-investments (ROI) on amount spend in employee development, training and welfare programs.

The Employee performance appraisal in specific and organizational performance management in general, is a farcical exercise in most corporate environments with very little emphasis on employee engagement and development. "The last remembered interaction" plays a significant role in determining employee rankings. Thus organizations forgo an important opportunity for employee evaluation and engagement and thereby enhancing its intellectual capital. Competency Quotient (CQ) provides an effective and consistent mechanism to evaluate organizational employees based on their core competencies (behavioural as well as technical), work experience and academic achievements. This can form the basis for planning suitable interventions to enhance employee morale, productivity and effectiveness.

Functioning

Competency Quotient (CQ) is a score derived from a combination of standardized tests including IQ & EQ, academic profiling, Behavioural Elicitation Interviews (BEI) and Competency Elicitation Interviews (CEI). CQ provides a consistent mechanism for ranking individuals within and across organizations, academic institutions across multiple domains. The median Full Scale CQ is centered at 100, with a standard deviation (SD) of 15. In a normal distribution, the CQ would range one SD above and below the mean (i.e., between 85 and 115).

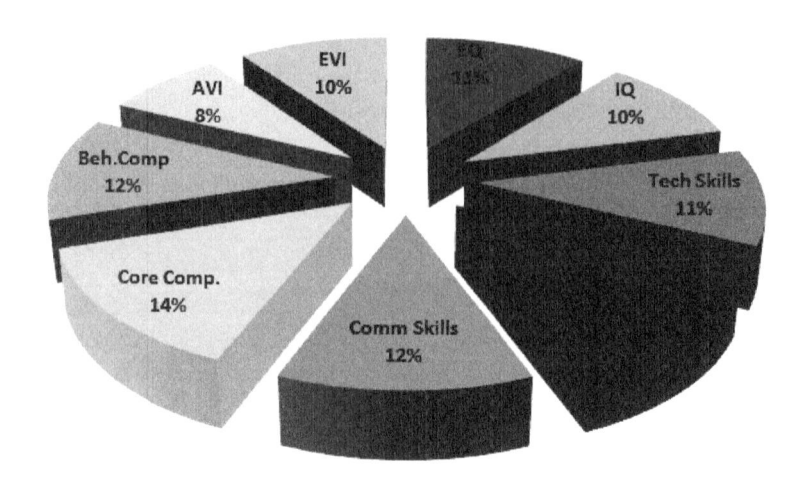

$$Competency\ Quotient\ (CQ) = \{0.08 * x_8 + 0.1 * (x_2 + x_9) + 0.11 * (x_1 + x_3) + 0.12(x_4 + x_5 + x_7) + 0.14 * x_6$$

Need & Benefits

CQ provides a holistic measure of an ascertaining the value of an employee to an organization irrespective of its operational domain. CQ can also be employed to grade fresh graduates being churned out by educational institutions. This is especially of immense value in the Indian subcontinent where there is a tremendous gap between academic curriculum and industry demands.

Figure 5 – Competency Quotient – Primary Constituents
The figure 5 illustrates the constituents of CQ. The Weightage of constituents is also included. The primary constituents are as listed under:
1. Emotional Quotient - EQ (x_1)
2. Intelligence Quotient - IQ (x_2)
3. Generic Technical Skills (x_3)
4. Management Skills (x_4)
5. Communicational Skills (Verbal & Written) (x_5)
6. Core Competencies (x_6)
7. Behavioural Competencies (x_7)
8. Academic Value Index – AVI (x_8)
9. Employment Value Index – EVI (x_9)

The mechanism of arriving at the CQ as well as the components of the primary constituents is listed in the following section. Table 2 lists down the rankings of the CQ constituents. The table is based on the analysis of primary data collected from over 800 respondents through online/offline surveys and interviews.

Table 2 – CQ - Ranking of Primary Constituents

Parameters	Rating Average (out of 6)
EQ	5.52
IQ	5.76
Technical Skills (Generic)	5.48
Management Skills	5.42
Communication Skills	5.72
Core Competencies	5.33
Behavioral Competencies	5
AVI	4.3
EVI	4.08

Emotional Quotient Estimation

Emotional Quotient (EQ) is the ability to sense, understand and effectively apply the power of emotions to facilitate high levels of collaboration and productivity at the workplace. EQ provides a better indication of success of an individual in their workplace as compared to Intellectual intelligence (IQ). EQ assessment is done by administering a questionnaire in a controlled environment.

Intellectual Quotient Estimation

Intellectual Quotient (IQ) assessment is based on a standard online questionnaire based test administered to participants in a controlled time environment. The standardized the WAIS-IV (2008) test is used for this purpose. WAIS-IV comprises of 10 core subtests and five supplemental subtests. The 10 core subtests comprises the Full Scale IQ. These tests includes the General Ability Index (GAI) comprising of questions based on similarities, Verbal Comprehension Index (VCI) based on vocabulary & information subtests and the Perceptual Reasoning Index (PRI) based on block design, matrix reasoning & visual puzzles subtests (Wikipedia, 2014).

Indices & Scales
There are four index scores representing major components of intelligence:
1. Verbal Comprehension Index (VCI)
2. Perceptual Reasoning Index (PRI)
3. Working Memory Index (WMI)
4. Processing Speed Index (PSI)

The intellectual abilities of an individual are summarized through two broad scores as listed under:
1. Full Scale IQ (FSIQ)
    - Based on the total combined performance of the VCI, PRI, WMI & PSI
2. General Ability Index (GAI)
    - Based only on the six subtests comprising VCI & PRI

Subtests

VCI includes four tests as listed under:
1. Similarities
2. Vocabulary
3. Information

4. Comprehension

PRI comprises of five tests as listed under:
1. Block Design
2. Matrix Reasoning
3. Visual Puzzles
4. Picture Completion
5. Figure Weights

WMI is derived from the following three tests:
1. Digit Span: The tests includes questions covering attention, concentration & mental control
2. Arithmetic: The tests includes questions covering concentration while manipulating mental mathematical problems
3. Letter- The tests include number sequencing, attention and working memory questions

PSI includes the following three tests:
1. Symbol Search – This test covers questions based on visual perception & speed
2. Coding - This subtest includes questions covering visual-motor coordination, motor responses and mental speed
3. Cancellation – This sub-test includes evaluation based on visual-perceptual speed

Technical Skills Evaluation

Technical skill evaluation is through an objective test administered electronically using a bank of questions and standardized scoring mechanisms are employed for assessment. There would be different tests for standard domains. Objective tests require a user to choose or provide a response to a question (multiple-choice, true-false, and matching items) whose correct answer is predetermined. Objective tests consists a mix of different question types. They are as listed below:
1. Select a solution from a set of choices (multiple choices, true-false, matching)
2. Identify an object or position (graphical hotspot

3. Supply brief numeric or text responses (text input)

Objective tests measure a candidate's ability to remember many facts and figures as well as their understanding of the subject being assessed. These tests are designed to make the candidate think independently and test their ability of high level critical reasoning and making fine discriminations to determine the best answer.

Management Skills Evaluation

Management skill evaluation is through an objective test administered electronically using a bank of questions and standardized scoring mechanisms employed for assessment.

Communication Skills Evaluation

Communication skill evaluation is through an objective test administered electronically using a bank of questions and standardized scoring mechanisms employed for assessment.

Core Competency Elicitation

Core competency elicitation is the process of listing, evaluating and verifying the core competencies of an individual using a variety of techniques including traditional, collaborative, cognitive and contextual approaches. These include interviews (open-ended as well as structured), surveys, questionnaires, participatory design, prototyping, task analysis, ethnographic techniques and standard knowledge acquisition techniques.

Behavioural Competency Elicitation

Behavioural competency elicitation is the process of listing, evaluating and verifying the core competencies of an individual using a variety of techniques including traditional, collaborative, cognitive and contextual approaches. These include interviews (open-ended as well as structured), surveys, questionnaires, participatory design, prototyping, task analysis, ethnographic techniques and standard knowledge acquisition techniques.

AVI Estimation

The Academic Value Index (AVI) is used to measure the academic credentials of an individual. The AVI by itself may not be an indicator of an individual's true value to an organization. AVI is comprised of six components and are as illustrated in the figure 6.

The Table 3 provides the weightages of individual components.

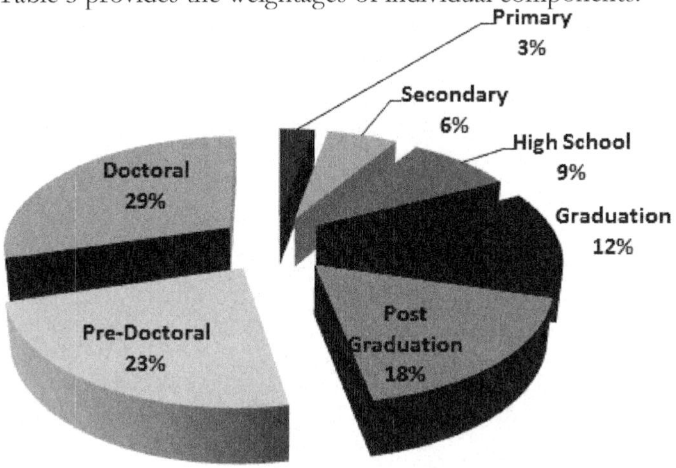

Figure 6 – Academic Value Index

Table 3 – Academic Value Index - Constituents & Weightage

S.N	Education	Weightage
1	Primary (y_1)	8
2	High School (y_2)	9
3	Graduation (y_3)	12
4	Post-Graduation(y_4)	18
5	Pre-Doctoral (y_5)	24
6	Doctoral (y_6)	29

Academic Value Index(AVI)
$$= \{0.08 * y_1 + 0.09 * y_2 + 0.12 * y_3 + 0.18 * y_4 + 0.24 * y_5 + 0.29 * y_6\}$$

EVI Estimation

The Employee Value Index (EVI) is a comprehensive index that is used to provide the overall value of an employee to a business enterprise. EVI can be used to rank employees within a business enterprise. It can be also be used to rank or compare a potential hire with the existing employees. This can have an important bearing on the manpower cost, identifying individuals with high talent and growth potential; suggest suitable interventions (monetary, job rotation, learning & development) besides a host of other applications. The table 4 below lists the key parameters constituting EVI and their respective weightages.

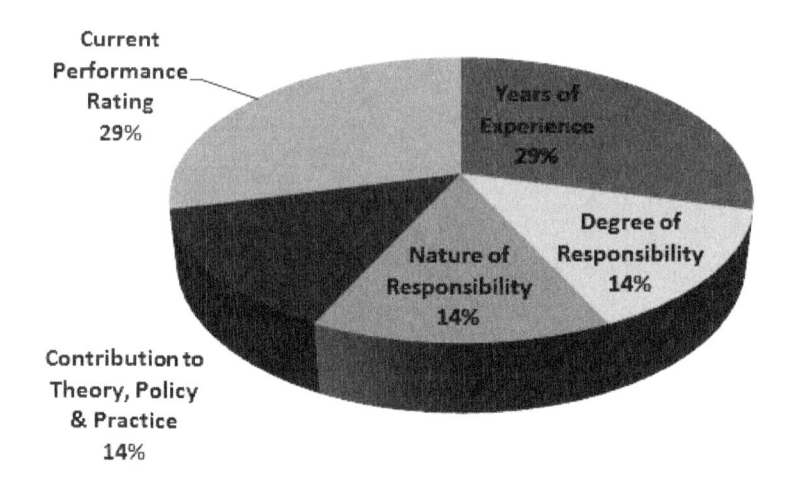

Figure 5 – Employment Value Index

Table 4 – Employment Value Index

S.N	Parameters	Weightage
A	Years of Experience	29
B	Degree of Responsibility	14
C	Nature of Responsibility	14
D	Contribution to Theory, Policy & Practice	14
E	Current Performance Rating	29
A	**Years of Experience**	
1	Exactly Same Profile (85-100%)	45
2	Mostly Matching Profile (55 -85%)	33
3	Slightly Matching Profile (35-55%)	18
4	Different Profile (0-35%)	4
B	**Degree of Responsibility**	
1	Support Staff	5
2	Executive Level	10

COMPETENCY QUOTIENT

3	Junior Management Cadre	15
4	Middle Management Cadre	21
5	Senior Management Cadre	23
6	Top Level Management	26
C	**Nature of Responsibility**	**Weightage**
1	Support	23
2	Operational /Field	32
3	Decision Making	45
D	**Contribution to Theory, Policy & Practice**	**Weightage**
1	Patents	25
2	Books Authored	25
3	Papers Presented (Conferences)	20
4	Papers Presented (Journals)	15
5	Others	15
E	**Current/Last Performance Rating**	**Weightage**
1	90 -100 %	41
2	75 -90 %	31
3	55 - 75 %	20
4	35 - 55 %	8
5	0 - 35 %	0

Employment Value Index (EVI)
$$= \{0.29 * (A + E) + 0.14 * (B + C + D)\}$$

Summary

Competency Quotient (CQ) – A score derived from a combination of standardized tests including IQ & EQ, academic profiling, Behavioural Elicitation Interviews (BEI) and Competency Elicitation Interviews (CEI). CQ provides a consistent mechanism for ranking individuals within and across organizations, academic institutions across multiple domains. The median Full Scale CQ is centered at 100, with a standard deviation (SD) of 15. In a normal distribution, the CQ would range one SD above and below the mean (i.e., between 85 and 115). CQ provides a holistic measure of an ascertaining the value of an employee to an organization irrespective of its operational domain. CQ can also be employed to grade fresh graduates being churned out by educational institutions. This is especially of immense value in the Indian subcontinent where there is a tremendous gap between academic curriculum and industry demands.

The Academic Value Index (AVI) is a score used to measure the academic credentials of an individual and thus estimate the potential value to an organization. AVI is comprised of six components that are used to rate the academic value of an individual.

The Employee Value Index (EVI) is a comprehensive score that is used to provide the overall value of an employee to a business enterprise. EVI can be used to rank employees within a business enterprise. It can be also be used to rank or compare a potential hire with the existing employees. This can have an important bearing on the manpower cost, identifying individuals with high talent and growth potential; suggest suitable interventions (monetary, job rotation, learning & development) besides a host of other applications.

KEY TERMS

Academic Value Index (AVI)
Behavioural Elicitation Interviews (BEI)
Competency Elicitation Interviews (CEI)
Competency Management (CM)
Competency Quotient (CQ)
Emotional Quotient (EQ)
Employment Value Index (EVI)
European Union (EU)
General Ability Index (GAI)
Human Capital (HC)
Intellectual Capital (IC)
Intelligence Quotient (IQ)
Key Result Areas (KRA)
Knowledge, Skills and Attributes (KSA)
Knowledge, Skills, Attitudes and Behaviours (KSAB)
Learning & Development (L&D)
On-The-Job Training (OTJ)
Perceptual Reasoning Index (PRI)
Return-On-Investments (ROI)
Standard Deviation (SD)
Training Need Analysis (TNA)
United Kingdom (UK)
United States of America (USA)
Verbal Comprehension Index (VCI)
Wechsler Adult Intelligence Scale – Fourth Edition (WAIS-IV)

REFERENCES

Bersin & Associates (2008). Organizational Talent Management. Retrieved July 1, 2010, from www.bersin.com.

Dubois, D. (Ed.) (1998). *The competency casebook*. Amherst, MA: HRD, & Silver Spring MD: International Society for Performance Improvement.

Gilbert, T.F. (1996). *Human Competence*. Silver Spring, MD: International Society for Performance Improvement.

Warier, S. (2003). Knowledge Management. Mumbai: Vikas Publishing House Pvt. Limited.

Wikipedia (2014). Wechsler Adult Intelligence Scale, Retrieved Sep 29, 2011 from http://en.wikipedia.org/wiki/Wechsler_Adult_Intelligence_Scale

INDEX

A

Academic Value Index, 12, 15, 16, 19
Attitude, 4, 8

B

Behavioural Competencies, 12

C

Communicational Skills, 12
Competence, 3, 4
Competence Versus Competency, 3
Competencies, 2
Competency, I, 2, 3, 5, 6, 10, 11, 15, 18
Competency Management, 3, 4
Competency Modelling, 2
Competency Quotient, I
Competitive Advantage, 1
Core Competencies, 12
Core Competency Elicitation, 15

E

Emotional Quotient, 12
Employee Value Index, 16
Employment Value Index – EVI, 12

F

Full Scale IQ, 13

G

General Ability Index, 13

H

Human Capital, 4, 8

I

Intangible Assets, 2
Intellectual Agility, 4
Intellectual Capital, 4, 7, 22
Intelligence Quotient, 12

J

Job Search, 5

K

Key Success Factors, 9
Knowledge Capital, 7
Knowledge, Skills And Attributes, 2

O

Organizational Value Chain, 7

P

Perceptual Reasoning Index, 13
Performance Appraisal, 10

R

Recruitment, 5, 10

S

Superior Performers, 2

T

Talent Management, 1
Training Need Analysis, 5

V

Verbal Comprehension Index, 13

ABOUT THE AUTHOR

Sudhir Warier is a Human Capability Management Coach with expertise in organizational knowledge management and a proven track record in developing and leading learning organizations. He has over 20years of experience with over 14 years in leading the Learning & Development and Human Capital Management function. He has hands-on experience in managing the entire organization Learning & Development and Human Capital Management value chain including training delivery (Corporate/Retail), academic management, curriculum development, R&D, Talent Management, Coaching and Mentoring. He has also spent over 15 years in the field of Knowledge Management (Intellectual Capital Management) engaged in research activities, developing organizational frameworks and assessing organizational competency management initiatives. He has authored seven books and published over 30 high quality research papers in international conferences and peer reviewed journals. His book titled 'Knowledge Management' is a best seller and a reference text for varied university degree and post graduate courses internationally.

OTHER PUBLICATIONS

S.N	Name	ISBN
1	Knowledge Management	978-8125913634
2	Data Warehousing Essentials	978-1463590482
3	Data Mining Fundamentals	978-1484145463
4	Optical Communication Fundamentals	978-1482615791
5	Strategic Management	-
6	Management Theory & Practice	-
7	Competency Management – The Conceptual Framework	978-1499236972
8	A Framework for Measuring Intangible Assets	978-1502869340
9	Competency Quotient	978-1502863454
10	Competency Mapping & Management – A Comprehensive Survey Report	978-1502870292

Printed in Great Britain
by Amazon